ALONG THE ROAD EVERYONE MUST TRAVEL

DANIELLE PAFUNDA

Distributed by Independent Publishers Group
Chicago

©2025 Danielle Pafunda

No part of this book may be used or reproduced in any manner without written permission except in the case of brief quotations embodied in critical articles and reviews. Please direct inquiries to:

Saturnalia Books
2816 North Kent Rd.
Broomall, PA 19008
info@saturnaliabooks.com

ISBN: 978-1-947817-80-7 (print), 978-1-947817-81-4 (ebook)
Library of Congress Control Number: 2024949034

Cover art and book design by Robin Vuchnich

Distributed by:
Independent Publishing Group
814 N. Franklin St.
Chicago, IL 60610
800-888-4741

◊ ◊ ◊

Contents

You go back to get your holy things when your skin has greater part sun than air and stop touching your bitter friends it's true once married I had to go to the underworld for a really long time after which I came to live above the biotoxic soil crust but not with you or anyone

When the earth begins dying faster than I can do cut the plastic band from where it identifies me limbed and counted then go ahead give my number to the horned god

I dwell in the road to the sea everyone travels and dwell in your house preparing to haunt you if I'm not doing much later and dwell on your face and if you don't aggrieve me I or my daughters might could come back

Even spring has nether gloom I climb its roof and check Orion's posture lean over lonely friend my head aches a shoulder

I turned thirty in wartime I turned forty in wartime stay you irritate my heart with distance until the present comes a sheet of pearls and moor's breath in a dry clime and I bedeck you

Burn benzoin the resin expands cardiopulmonary fibers the resin weights sorrow while you get high the feeling of funeral grasses too

Everyone tells me there's no work on this road I make bad choices okay fine but I swing from a godswell and take a punch like a philomel

I fall asleep waiting for a call from the tribunal waiting for the elders to get here with their sacrificial blade I fall asleep before I die I want more dreams

A hot breeze comes up from the desert and blows my bullfaced tender friend back down the road to the sea I put my arms out I get the breeze like wings and my fluted heart goes sirens

Once in a while I mistake beauty for chaos and go whirling dusk mirror sadness but even then it is extraordinarily welcome clasping hands so don't forget me I don't forget you

Fast by the wide and dismal gates of hell I slowmo consider my claws frontgold base done jammed with vernal strife even the equinox uneasy for diggers

Where sound forms a bowl in the green my beloveds congregate and tho a drone scripts threat overhead we reap balm ash damp clover it's true time has eighty feet of handwoven rope in its satchel

Survey the demolishing current then in response feed the muscular fabric of love hand over hand far reach skeins that silk the terrain and therein we don't get anxious to own each other any longer I just want to drive and talk all night and feel this landscape breathe in my overswell

Don't say you love if that love will then try to exit the gates when I was unexpectedly released from the underworld I couldn't imagine an orpheus I couldn't float I could only cling to my home

Hold my wrist hold my ankle hold my tongue hold my mouth in your mouth and tell me things singular and windcrossed tell me murder and tell me future they're spelled the same

My tender friend thinks I live dangerously but says no it's not the breast full of scorpions nor the lack of income it's the way I leap into the arms of the gods sure they'll catch me no I say I'm not sure I'm never sure

My bullfaced tender friend was right about everything I consume one nasturtium after another wishing I'd been alive when first found

I ducked into a sympathetic pleiades and before I knew it neither desert nor sea stopped where the mountains started

Do not acknowledge you love lest it claw from you your body where I live in the desert but am always wet I wept for my home just a hole

Hurts to arrive in you and hurts to go you made me softer than I was a habitable dirt for all sorts of flourish I'm not hating on salvations I'm just calling out

Free salmacis from bodies not hers and free the mirror from its rocky wall and free the sand from its bound service grief a pearl my wealth is pearls then they dissolve

With all their space compressed such that they are purestar hunters they can be stretched inside me I envelope them a red envelope of radical dust

You go back to get your holy things when your skin has greater part sun than air and stop touching your bitter friends it's true once married I had to go to the underworld for a really long time after which I came to live above the biotoxic soil crust but not with you or anyone

two-shaped, ivy-covered, twice-kindred / feast / eat something / a partition / and watch yourself come back to life / a life / whose door is guarded by seabird / froth your skin, kick to shore

or

I wasn't a sea creature, nor drowned / I was / lover, I came to the sea and demanded entry to the borderless places because they shift, they aren't territory, I asked to leave / my nation state, I asked to be bride dissolved, to be sick and then / well, on shore I couldn't explain that my heart was a hospital in a hospital gown in a hospital, I couldn't explain / that pain was sex and one has only both / when you had me, I couldn't explain what I had done / with that / done with the way I had to encounter my name shaped on the public tongue

or

my name was / I left my holy things at the gibbous ridge and climbed over, keeping everyone alive with my ability to turn flesh to milk / I was not, myself, considered holy, then / it was obvious that I was just doing my job / I cooled your hot spirit with / materialism / it wasn't / me, I came in on a raft, I dove off the prairie, I alone, I swam all those miles to the sea, passing no other sea, passing / through every gate, gatehouse, and checkpoint, each / time my heart, lonely whale in a bone cavern, wet ossuary, starved-out, strung up, there / was so much air and so little oxygen, I breathed you in through a golden straw, I spun / your hair to gold, to reed, to straw, how pliant

or

don't talk to gods, don't put your ear to the source / code / switches shell to biome to spell / don't read aloud the formula of a virus if you don't want to be a virus / don't vow and sing / all night / your friends were on the velvet crest of a spring-damp hill and their names were just / sitting there, fresh / animals stole away the night / cells released from your gown and rails from so many syringes, you lost count, I / mean I / I lost count, the needle had been in me such a long time, and then I / went under, I / didn't have the agriculture to ask where I'd been / no longer had to answer my phone, nor to anyone, not with my name, at least not correctly, any longer, anything other than that: yes, I was down there / longer / harpies came out of my ribcage and sometimes a species would drip from above, where people / killed it / machines / and bad ideas, sometimes / a gust of hot wind through the line, though my lines were dead / I shut magic's face so it wouldn't call my name / I shut it like a box you can fuck with, but you can't

When the earth begins dying faster than I can do cut the plastic band from where it identifies me limbed and counted then go ahead give my number to the horned god

whitegrief hospital, magic gone, succeeded by rope of knotted levers, I mean lovers / lovers, oracular and gone / the window contracts on the bed as does a glove in covenant with the neat pad of a lover's palm, blooming / from a channel to either side, I / used to deaden this channel with a wreath of chants, but we didn't call them that / we called them conversations, we called them meetings, and I came to the table, repeatedly, both feast and festival, faux and thrust / thrust up / split like swan, swilled, spitted like froth from the god's sea-bearing mouth that's not / a god, that's an aperture, an organ in the earth's hide and she's hidden there, buttery skin, lodged and invisible to your eye, my eye, the night eye of unholy nurses and their holy charge, the you of the bed / I gave you my number and washed my face, splashing wine from my bullfaced tender friend's chalice / that is, something really common, a serviceable vessel with a crown of fruit flies

or

where you cum, lonely, unsad in your own / palm underneath / all that capitalism, I grow soft, in harmony with hard times, I / grow softer seeing you / in the company of tender friends who admire you / it's okay to get awed again / how long / did you burn memory's fiber-optic line thinking I'd see it

or

someone like me, hair swept from her neck, an epic, mobile beauty aging into the previously unknowable where beauty now runs to ruin in the very seat of its preservation / that is, we preserve it long enough to see it crumble, we preserve it so / there weren't fires raging enough to burn out that pretty youth of mine / just time / I age as a demeter does, no trains, no flower, no drugs, no long swims, you can't / swim there, now / you can't find anywhere good to die once the pastoral has been stripped / copper from its green / vein, you can't find / anywhere good to die, so you just get older, maybe change the channel, you're / the channeler, after all

or

you open up your browser, one day, and there's a valve through which a slow drop of rose absolute makes syrup / oil so old, an amber, feminine patience, which is to say / none / in the sly language of gender that fabricates normcore mortals, I / catch my daughter / microwaving a bone china dish full of raw crystals and I guess I have charge of a woman, now / I am fertility begetting fertility and chaos / a material war on particles and patience / every day / we measure and, every day, they're infinite wanting / every day must include pain, this bride whose veil we assemble, don't / call here if you don't want me to come running, I gave my number to this god and that god, I seared my number into a lot of skin, stall doors, heroic odes, and hymns, plus stuff I wrote / you can get my number there / in the book / I got in the bath, an invocation

or

a vocation / I could do both, and then ride you to the earth's core / my own core, not in my possession, well / deep

I dwell in the road to the sea everyone travels and dwell in your house preparing to haunt you if I'm not doing much later and dwell on your face and if you don't aggrieve me I or my daughters might could come back

When you go to the door of the sea god's house, also / my house, a place I dwelled / guarded / by a seabird who doesn't stop for pain, who / heats fire rocks in a trash dugout / drops hots into your gut, a cooked meal that bakes you from the inside, and / parts each blind's holy hide, a / nightbird who cocks the moon until it's soft and shoots it into you, a syringe-mouthed, glistening, jelly moon potion shot into your coal heart / like a bubble / a songbird stacking sand notes / taking notes / flushed countenance / says bird: this guy's wreck and mealsome, says: garbage like a chime that brings / brings, bearings, rings / all the birds to the yard

or

I won't go down / when you come / my face, guarded door where I keep time, I / keep time lashed like a daughter and trade her for my actual daughter standing in the ditch by the road to the sea everyone must travel, I / don't want her to obey you, and I don't / want her / to obey me, I want her to be a bad daughter, all legs, climbing / out of the squabbleoven and over the crust of a crater bored into earth, do not bore my daughter

or

she will flay you / she unspools a strip of time, the poisoned peel, she doesn't eat it / wiser than I at her age, by her age / I / had a husband / had to spit my red mouthfuls at his guests' feet, my / chores included serving them my unguarded smile and ungirding my hospitality without / enjoying the congress or its session, I hid / war wore my knees, but not for him, lace habit / in this shaft of time, I'm laced in / in revolution around my daughters, my bad habits, every day / this belief that pain must be included in / my greedy hold on time's mealy core, slowcore, sadcore revolution of flesh that can't keep juice, so turns rugged and greasy stewed hard winter venison, a long-ago husband double fisting antler and throat

or

this leather game falls back in the sand / if you don't want to go to the underworld, go underwater / no hot god will fool you going deep out in salt laters where the ribbed / gown / of sea tides, salt-stiff white bridal habit worn by / you call out nun, acolyte, you call them / daughters and they turn off their phones, I can't / remember how men got my number after I gave it up on the makeshift altar / altered it / on my knees, a dull classic / ropes saying the grace of each knot, forbidding beautiful images, lined up for record, and by the time / they turn / their turn / to come, beauty's convulsions give over to something we don't recognize

or

fertile sound of wave that carries wreck on rock, irritating your ear where birds wheel / too close by / checking you for doneness / done in / give up

or

I don't want this for you, I wanted to give you sight through a new lens / mine / drilled, cut deep, absorbing / you bathing, unusual visage from the rocks, I observe your flesh before birds, splintered vessels and rusted shafts, race / my face / opening against your dryfire skin and the refraction of salt's infinite crystal patina / auric from any angle, I had my arm out, coated in raw jewels, pulsing with favor, humming your favorite, not too worried about / who has frankincense, who has benzoin out here on the weary hippie road, preserving sage verbena, hardy mint, lavenders, sticky / in your crook, shush

or

if you don't want to go to the underworld, go out to the desert, and don't look / look / like that / look back at me, your eyes smoked four nights, two crystals sewn deep in the mountain's hot thigh, I take / a beak for a needle and tear out the stitches / what the fuck happened to you, I thought you were born, I thought we were / on / earth, I thought this must be the place, but it had a false pedestal through which / time / the holler guarded by, you know, guarded

or

so fucking many winged wheels of fortune bearing each the premonition of its own body, relic, and maybe / mine / own death, my handler, thereafter, you / don't get to die and lie down, but get to be ravaged again by the wild hospital

or

salt and deep dirt loosed to the murder wind was just feeling / some other person put up / your skin against mine, teach me the true fact of hugging, let me know / no, show / show me how it's okay to have run the length of the road to the sea and then the length of / your body in my arms / restrained against the ground, perform for me the embrace so I / don't break it / break against / this shaft, and go down / this astonishing shaft, the mechanism by which time swallows, does / it to us / each time my daughter calls / home / a movie / she says, sorry, mama, you / don't get an invitation to the house of the dead exes, weeping salt on the inlet, its mouth a'foam with rocks, without falling down that shaft, you / don't have to get it yet, you'll know us forever, we're ore

Even spring has nether gloom I climb its roof and check Orion's posture lean over lonely friend my head aches a shoulder

where you stud your huntsman's belt, where you carry with you the burden words for celestial bodies, exit / no / I grab at, I grasp night air, almost a yard of damp fiber I ache to braid into rope, it's lasso, it / is the O quite large enough to encompass, but still tightly behold / does my O tolerate the stars' loose sword, and their heat as well / I wasn't kidding, I was / knowing / I knew a lot about softening to capacity, and then / the belief that every day must include pain / might sometimes be hypnotized, fledgling, speckled sand between thirsty junipers, fluttering hurt / new hurt / new, say it again, spell it, say it in the careless raked mirror / fresh down-like fur / pull my daughter's hair so she'll know how not to live

or

crash my body on some rocks, I chill and / call my father / to mind, I really loved him not / because he was a god a lot of people knew / he was a god / he was there when I was born of woman and the gold crud that issued from his / joy / I have always made men joyful, then disappointed them / their arms, their hilts, the dates of their hilts, jilted I was / never so / jilted, I made them dislike me, capsize me, I swam home, deep through thick crust layers of home, you / think it's solid, but then you soften against the ground while the ground softens against you / underground, the day under the grave, under the meadow that shifts its weight beside the road to the sea that everyone must travel, beside the river ferries, the murder wind, the mountain scree running / down my cheeks / crumble, a slew of things keep going back to stone / get stoned / wonder if anyone loves you like: does anyone love me the way I want to feel it, right now / the sun / doesn't burn this place down and change its name, despite all the shit we talk about it / getting darker, now, but the harbor's fluttering eyelids don't mean sleep, they / pick a tarantula off the low beam where ceiling meets habitat / sin / ride a little pony all the way to town, clasp fur to cheek, clasp hands not clap, no one / wants your praise / tonight, it's a quiet ode for us who got no nurses on duty, the stillwhite failure of skin and bone, a long song I'm singing hardwrong with my hands up / up / up the back of your shirt, buttons taking / I'm not willing to spend time here, but neither am I sure where to take you, it turns out / every party is a sacrifice, my tender friends / my thighs are shook where empty, my cup comes back filled with a bright taste I'm certain / I like it / in my name is salt, in my tender friends' names the dusk, we come / from the center and we sell destined labor

or

charm them with your fleet and stylish charms, charm me, think about—without wanting to—how easy to / too easy, it would be / to burn yourself among sleepers, not care if anyone dreams your name into the whorl while a crummy band lights up and your people lay out to either side, a channel of how you were and become remembered, remembering / none of that is here / now, a cult you member / I've got my hands up and what looks like prayer might as well reach / into the dirt to grab my wrist and I'll grab yours back and haul, and haul, like hell

I turned thirty in wartime I turned forty in wartime stay you irritate my heart with distance until the present comes a sheet of pearls and moor's breath in a dry clime and I bedeck you

trade my centaur in the garden for a minotaur on the cliffs, my siren in the sea for a circe on the rocks, and my mirrors for those shards between the mixed rust media and things we chucked there kicking sunlight up the dunes, dead to us from their final starpit expiration / merciless between my ribs, the huntress's golden barb enters me, enters the room through me, how'd we / get inside, I don't know if it'll pierce you too, thick hide, fur, muscle bound like a book of the dead / smells lush and smart in the bombed-out desert library, but look there, the center of the lyric reflects your horns, carved calcium-ridged rings, smoke-blackened your dusking horns, and I don't know / if they'll both / pierce me, I'm done being whole

or

pupils askew, harmony leaking wetly lilting, my lips gone mytho-red as a killbeach promise, byronic and vampy in the / face / my face a lyric ode to gutter chance / my bullfaced tender friend knows my bones, Artemis knows my target, my flesh weeps over all this knowledge, a processional / round up the years to forty / forty-million rocks, hard things where once were disparate movements, electric horizons, cunning thread

or

an old name autocorrected teaches your phone to bone a god and wait here for the god's reply a / god-hung legacy cruises night's wet field, you / start your ode dear one, dear / when you start your ode what up, you start to say I just can't get enough, so push it / into me / the wave, I was / wild before and after a husband

or

this astralwoven spike juts out of my ribcage, but it isn't bloody, it isn't / glowing, many-fingered organ of ever-more-outer space, receiver of exile, sorrow, a homing device, I'm not / your home, you devise, I'm trying / to get better at things, I list the shell reports / for my sons and daughters and children, I got you / into this, you've bombed them, I / lift / the hide on the day and usher everyone under, huddle, here, in anthroanimalia, in body warmth, in the furnace, put / a vata in charge and you'll get what you pay for, a hot pulse from the mountain's white fever, pulses that descend cliffs, visible alterations of heat and pressure washing scree into the horned god's eyes, heal them / with salt, it stings like new again / sting your shaft, stinged-open mine, sting mineral deposits until lit they light this bull's face, I / don't have any incense, I didn't put that guy's number in my phone, who / am I to press a moth's wing to dust, lace my lips and part my lips as I have / always done / not a girl, a daughter, a wife, but / a demeter, not / a pain goes by / on the road, the reluctant, persistent road to the sea that passes by the hospital that everyone, even the ferryman, must travel

or

I won't tell you which mirror is yours / between brides' thighs, a pagan search-and-rescue / check your torn-to-ribbons pockets, bleeding, give me all your money and dash / the dash in your car reads anchor midnight, the road carries foot traffic, beasts speed, and how fast sea to cliff to moor to me, a nursery rhyme warning, warming, wartime tattle coming faster, now and you / won't feel shame when the ring through your wet snout gets hooked to my clit, and spite then split from me

Burn benzoin the resin expands cardiopulmonary fibers the resin weights sorrow while you get high the feeling of funeral grasses too

Artemis with cadenced hands / hands me a long pipe, carved ornate, thru which smoke wanders crossing corneal night, dilating pupils / softening / unmirroring pressure points from rigid ricks of light, the light supposedly unmoored, in fact fixed, of the mind, cold and planetary, agape to inky voids and Orion's / belt unslung, unclear if he's coming, too

or

going / a plague of spidery strangers flies by, dismissive husks in the gutters, gross algorithm for every type of want, for / getting sound and picture out of people, but nothing else, a couple weeks past equinox, and / all the lovers marco-polo each other, indifferent to the colony at this lilac hour

or

like I'm sitting alone with a lot of math / mathematical mistakes / make me / the ink between velvet sheath and altar stack, the white rust wreck of someone / who came / before me, someone who would've hit you hard to make you hard and keep you safe as / the stump where you used to burn shit you stole, cigarettes and copper wire bundled into bright cables that, until you stole them, spelled out people's names, spelled sorry I'm late, it's for real this time, mom's dead / business cards and fake IDs, phone numbers in the napkin era, you're afraid of going back to the snow, it's / okay / so am I / as houses

or

feeling up in a back booth doesn't feel any different than hauling your weary feelings one more time down the chronic road to the door guarded by a seabird who remembers / every day the belief, from sea to desert, must include / pain / the road, the only lover who remembers what you look like parting your O mouth, signs surprise, issues smoke / you swiped / you lit / lifted / your veil freely / I mean what did you really need to say to the bloated nettles or spiked surf, am I / describing them precisely enough for you because I can / do that / if you want / a resolution and its bitter feelings, I can give you / both / I can / say salt, say fat stinging bed of possibility, take me, burn anything / once / and its name sweeps your tongue, your tongue sweeps mine, I feel a crater's worth of star and bone go off / take me back to the mycelium highway, mark your way / burn / these ribbons, my seven-chakra hair, and carry on into dronetime

or

a word needn't be gentle to soften, to carry, I / gave away and received in return my monogamy, which wasn't anything / it wasn't me, at all / I was proud of my solitude and territorial for reasons other than wanting to get fucked whenever I wanted, presuming I was a piece, presuming someone wanted me, taking my manse lease like juliet the failed heroine, tragic hero / jupiter the failed sun, jupiter witchbaby in brineland, who didn't want to dazzle, but talk to you / I, too, wanted to talk to you until talk were a fuck that went eighty years deep / that is, don't sell a planet if you don't yet know its name

or

maybe / it talks to your liver, and then who are you going to be when you cannot keep up with the suction of a long-needled century / brewing dandelion tisane, in this particular instance it's not an act of poverty, but right next to impoverishment where / strangers came off the road and presumed any persephone a vessel that owed them service, so didn't catch the inky unknown between her rounded lip and whetted one

or

beheld, so, fuck it, embrace me I could use some / it isn't every night because I would / never do that to you / burn benzoin and share a feeling

Everyone tells me there's no work on this road I make bad choices okay fine but I swing from a godswell and take a punch like a philomel

no more shame / for my failures, as beads, I read them off full of grace, I jerk them off / the fine jet string that stringed them from cleft to / trouble / trouble me, I've been down in the sand with Artemis, with sticks / the women can draw their waves and silence / write the names of roadside fleabag attackers so boring, lazing there, waiting for a power surge, waiting until a light goes on above the tits, below the eyes, in the pathetic grottoes, men / keep piling up against the gutter / does the sea have a gutter, you want to know / yes / guttering against your thigh same as it does continent, as it does the future pearl that'll come of this champagne flute shattering against the deck, its shards a bridal spray of white cutting / ships, men, palaces, bars, funeral tops, literature bottoms, everything seems / unattainable, today, but the voice on the line, the bullfaced voice that broke out of husbandry

or

use salt to conduct your voice through copper wire / it turns the wire the gold of the gold dust woman who collects fibers from your voice, repurposes them for sonic paintings, loud thrashes of paint roil, smell like verbena and bonebrute / men do it, too, and those beyond the binary, exchanging grosgrain for fuckface, it's / so boring, we're laughing again / hard / and mercy feelings come upon me, I have so many friends I never write songs about, it's / okay to remember you love some, it's okay to go soft places in you're hard, who's / that on the road, now, a philomel comes typing up a storm she's made of talking, made of this dishonest belief that every day / might divest / some pain, she / has seven braids in her fist, she cut them from beasts of the field, soldiers, and sad moms, I / point her out to my daughter I / point to her lit-afire sandals and the weeping sash she tows, it's / okay to be in love, I tell my daughter, it's okay, it doesn't have to last long

or

I'm so sorry I'm not singing your name, screaming, singeing, freaking out your name on a rooftop, clifftop, overlooking the deadeye of a new-moon sea / what / it's a full moon courting jupiter, the failed sun, who won't go back home to father, won't hide his face, looks side-eyed, sweet enough at my hide, asks every question real slow like we're not going anywhere, he asks what'd you do with your bullfaced tender friend, where'd you send the harpy with the hawk's eye, the / centaurs and stags leap over the hedge of a rich man's house I can see clearly from the tidal pool, and well enough when I'm orbit-slung in my bed in the desert, I / try to fix up all this garbage / I'm not the first poet to try, but maybe I'm the first one to catalog / every day, pain fluxes its material through the morning sky, then stalls by evening / stall with me, awhile / I'm your bed-down, I'm your hay and brushes, I'm a minor classical figure, and also a major / force shifts the atmosphere, visible as an h-bomb, visible as a reflection / that is, the reflection traverses the room, visits its surfaces and slips away, maybe / I'm so lovely today, the reflection ambushes you on its course, and then we're a new thing, they'll give us a bull's name, they'll call me / derivative, maybe / I'm so lovely, I can't get caught by silverbacks or reflecting pools, or your sticky / stretch of luck that runs the salt road everyone must travel, it / doesn't get you off the ferry, it doesn't get you on the ship, the rocks

or

I fall short of land, this day, and strike your name in water / what is more, the water takes its gold flume of pleasure, says don't cry, trash, you're home, girl

I fall asleep waiting for a call from the tribunal waiting for the elders to get here with their sacrificial blade I fall asleep before I die I want more dreams

unbleached, we demeters stand in line at sunset, and beside me loudly sobbing one says each day this belief must contain us, this we that's composed of previously whole persons, the mythology that there are previously / whole people / goldfields, blazing star, ghost flower by the side of the road from the desert to the sea, but deep in the desert, this time, deep in the crux, not where there's beach glass tossed on sunwave, but where there's no answer and it's late and the women in this line are getting scared / I'm scared / I say to the demeter next to me who smells of jasmine, cumin, and salt

or

I don't say anything because I don't want Artemis to overhear me breaking covenant, I / didn't / I promise to wear my spine a shield and my breast a breastplate, didn't I take the long horns of that tender friend in my whetstone hands and say sharpen / at night, I climb the rise and lean my forehead against Orion's cool, flat sword, I don't / hunt, I don't fish, I don't host, I know / my birth / the day is somewhere around here, so I don't even dare breathe, tonight / I want off the road and out of the moon's light, out of history's red tide, breathe out

or

I fish around for the salt god's number and invoke him in a bath of electrolyte tears / fuck me, I beg / fuck my life / take the bare spot on a bird's chest and liken it to my losses easily foretold, easy in the hand, so hard to slip the scalpel to / whoever was in there, who left her familiar lashed to the bed, wasn't me, wasn't my daughter, I / tell my daughter don't start crying or you'll / never stop crying / don't give your number out to gods, and when you go back to hades, go quiet and lone / sometimes / I'm on the road deep in the desert where sunlight breaches my breastbone, the only protection I took, I wasn't thinking clearly when I packed my bag, I packed things I didn't / need / don't fit in with the salt god's retinue of beautiful people

or

on the road everyone must travel, the belief that every day must include pain becomes / gothic / a cholla lace desert veil, the antiqued eyes of chicory, no matter how / old, a bloom fans its tail out across waxbacked beetle tracks, and I can hear a demeter singing, now, you came from heaven / come into me / you came / from heaven and / came into me, I / wanted to go to her, I / became a place in the desert, I ran / the road to the sea and back, I / wasn't / stopped by any wet god, I wasn't startled by any star set careless on the rise, a veined bloodrock burning alongside it in sympathy, and, so, I was burning, too / every day must include a we that were once presumed separate and whole / wholeheartedly, I can't sing any longer, my voice caves, I take a punch / a sea-cut glass of stinging nectar and mayfly, I / don't have fine things any longer, I have fine thoughts

A hot breeze comes up from the desert and blows my bullfaced tender friend back down the road to the sea I put my arms out I get the breeze like wings and my fluted heart goes sirens

some days are more cursed than others, though every day must contain this belief that pain must / include itself / a snub-nosed star gives me everything I need right now, and nothing I need later / like I need money and time, I / need to know how to spell your name, kissed out of me by numbers, kissed off my lips by other names less bedecked in flowers and blister / blisterbacked beetle, head as waxen as a purim mask, legs working against quartz, you're my sapphire keep / says the centaur to his host / you're my string of gems I spill across a seabed, pearls-cum-travels rich friends pass along / the road everyone must travel / brings me / repast / I wouldn't otherwise eat, recline, I'm trying so hard to stay out of the nervous white failure, I don't even want to say I / remember / remember the aquarium of an afternoon I put myself inside for safekeeping /safekeep/ put your head against my innermost / my friend / tender friend who has a bull for a father and transgressions for mother

or

you can't say anyone's name in the road without them showing up lit and starferal, I know you / call this sadness, and the copper-tinged scent is also a type of sadness, memory, wet hide bind / me, hands down, so I can't push pleasure back from me, bind my ankles so tonight I don't walk the road, I / sleep / in a seabed and receive a gush of gems with good grace, though I'm terrified I won't remember my way back when they wash me out / to sea / to sand / neither place is really where I live, where I live is / on the road everyone must travel from the desert to the sea / a salt flat, a sea-salt spell, a siren stings your muzzle, she kisses from you my name, your name, the fat names of stars, of gods from the illustrated index of wild-growing gods, beetles, caterpillars, doves, and startled innkeepers fretting the linen and fretting time just / keeps bringing us new travelers / kisses your name from my mouth as I'm coming to, leaning hard, giving my throat to Orion, I / climb up the roof after everyone's gone and I'm stuck here alone / here / I give him my throat for his starry sword, a whetstone flesh and / song and / okay, I'll be a woman tonight, I took that name from history as daughter, wife, a demeter, turned it fleshside and said okay / I did often settle / for what was near to hand

or

other times, my hand was extended across the chasm in case you ever wanted to hold it in your velvet fieldmouth, and in case something should fall into it I wouldn't otherwise have known, I / always took the bow though I was / not hungry, sad and listening to the ceremony rise up the hill, I / listen to it once in metal, then once in silk, I lay down my linens and give most of my trousseau back to the sea god, this is why we can't have anything nice / gods don't play / I tell my daughter / be nice to me but don't be / nice to anyone / else / even travelers / be sure you get off the road / the road is for the likes of me, who's not / waiting at the door to the house guarded by a seabird, no one / keeps me waiting at home, the fires going round on the neighbors' backs, and the smoke funnels dove-gray down, soft, choke, I lean / my throat into the palm / I give my throat and keep

or

I keep very little, now / everything rusts and wears thin / I think about the lush bride I once saw / my reflection in the bottomless tide pool that goes down to hades and back up to daddy, rhyming the spell / everyone's name, here, on the road, put back / my head, so that my throat gives you the sign of a tender friend, more / surprising when you lean your head against my innermost, most copper-dovetail self, don't ever / let me be unkind / to you, don't ever let my throat / go / rushing back down the road from the desert to the sea / travel it twice, you get less mortal each time

Once in a while I mistake beauty for chaos and go whirling dusk mirror sadness but even then it is extraordinarily welcome clasping hands so don't forget me I don't forget you

ivy-covered tender friends with golden lashes sweeping scored-bare faces, turned up loud so they can hear each other interrupting the monotonous grief / happens because what happens when you have more feelings than hours, you / step out on the road everyone must travel where I'm already walking the dusky back and forth, my oversized heart knocking me off balance, I recover a goat's step and love / isn't governed like the sea or the hunt / love, ungovernable and shadowed most nights, I can't feel any company or find my list of immortal familiars / salt blows in from the coast and other ions radiate from the ground up, turn / the light out, and lie / still, my heart grows vast and remembers how to print its own pig name

or

I get so lonely, I complain to Orion stuck in that obvious place hardly anyone bothers to look / for him, there, with his belt and sword, I place my hand on his burning boot / boot me out into the night and I'll just hunt for love, I'll take a dagger to pin it down and won't come home till morning / take my gown from me and leave me naked at the foot of the godsmount, the bed, Orion's boots / stall me / once more wasting time and money, a young girl / comes back from the sea, one hand frozen around the neck of a small dog, her free hand gropes along the road for those dark needles and the bow / bends against my throat, I lean into that dark / needle stitch / my head rolls off my throat and I stitch it back inexpertly, the sun- / drenched god tells me what's so clearly wrong with my hopes and dreams, and / my echostep on the road where it approaches the sea cliffs / take all sound out of the clanging visitor, and visit me, there, among caterpillars whose thick black bodies and gold punctures readily spill

or

try again to dazzle me, keep changing our lives, I / don't live here, so I don't have to / live anywhere, my bullfaced tender friend knows where to find me, my daughter knows how to / find me / I'm guarded by a seabird, and I'm making my bed in the night's nest, I / bestow my body on nightground, spiders tick over my skin, and my phone goes off with a thousand dark needles pointing to my throat / my home is in my throat, I feel especially / lonely, it doesn't / mean you / didn't / love me / I scream up at Orion, in a bad mood, knowing he's immovable and grateful he won't tell anyone I think about packing my bags, getting off this road, maybe walking out into the desert without my phone, without my friends who believe in laws and crested beauty, who bed down together in that certain, secret scheme of night I haven't / accessed / so, I spell my pig name, my old name, my flesh name, my throat with my voice, call myself chapel, call myself tongueless bird, daughter once whispering night's plans to a lover whose starcold ear turned heavenward, tuned / out / one night, no one calls

or

I know you treasured me, and I you, before I got so petty into time and money, not because I had any / where else / to go, I just / got impatient looking at the white lull of my past and the slick teeth of my future, Artemis's grin, everything bit too near the quick belief that every day must include pain / and so must I / forever, it became a familiar hymn, until my bloodred throat was just the metaphor for noise, and blood was just the metaphor for someone who'd outlived her brideliest days / there was / no such thing as / the human heart / in love, there was no beating out gold leaf spilling over poppies, spilling across the road from desert to sea, the poppies visible from space / gods living vast miles up and underworld / walk all night while silent Orion keeps the tip of his sword pointed neatly beneath my shoulder blade, I / rely on so many types of weapon to point me / the dusky needle / my mirror for how I move, not north and up, but in and innermost

or

it's the only place to stay on the road and the travelers hate it / it / feels wrong, they can tell / each other all about it, but they don't know / the worst part is that it was built by hand / by my hands / possessed / callused from bowstring, frostbit from starfucking, an actuary underworld equation, pure math sullied by temper and dislike / I know so many numbers, but none of them solve for me the problem of where I might go when I stop traveling this road, neither dying nor returning / the dead / an undertow pulls the hem of my gown, says go walking, I / take off through aster and veiny moonflower, I suck / a briny bloom / your thick heart, you love me and, heart, you love me, you / texters and gods who loved me by turns, then loosed me, I remember / your pig names, spell them up to Orion, this heavenly sorrow running my blood to silver over a new-moon grave, replacing the moon with me, giving me the taste for skin memory, giving me a heart like a vault for when all other riches go / water like a million mashed up diamonds / fled / flood from me

Fast by the wide and dismal gates of hell I slowmo consider my claws frontgold base done jammed with vernal strife even the equinox uneasy for diggers

illustrious, horned, and of bountiful mind when I approach the gates, I become tall, a ship's mast announcing her own return / sailors live, sailors dead, don't make a big deal, it's not the living whose starry petals part thorn from stem from / your face riven, my way of parting gates when the last of life's blood hitches through, as when your mouth is warm and I cannot tell if you like me or not, but you're there, my / horned god says go for it, you're dying, my hymnal says / I should try / I cannot / tell if you like me, I'm laughing a mouthful of meteors

or

I'm curled up against Orion's indifferent sack of captures / to be hunter or hunted is nothing, it's only the hunt itself that isn't already dead or trapped or covered in hide, that is, buried in kill / I am / parted, imperfect, waiting for the gates to sluice, waiting to get welcomed into the next room, I / go silent, waiting / for guests are unpredictable and tilt the floorboards, tilt even this concrete slab, the desert anchor, every ship atop its wave holding still enough, and I / loosen my politics for a second, lower my veil of tears, loose salt from my palms, pour out black salt wings with / no loft, they catch the light, even when I stand alone on the roof, everyone else gone back to sea or bed / the seabed / were they pretty / Orion doesn't ask / yes they were pretty / they were the gods of disappearance, gods of lush mouth and heavy hand, no one could see them from the ground, until I took aim

or

I walked the road seaward for the feast, I took my gold cuffs that keep my voice down, I combed the poison out of my lashes, I lashed to my breast a plate of knitted hours so that I might not / forget the way home, my keep, I keep / my daughter there, but it isn't / home, I sing the easy tide of doing and weaving, but it isn't / home, I try to leave it sincere in the knowledge of its anchor, its contract with the sand, its agreement to stay put under juniper, and jupiter, and, then I / send a couple texts to boost my spirits, fuck me, love me, kmn, and then I'm so deep in the road, fellow travelers mistake me for one of its / pebbles / I'm looking for tender / for my tender friends who will recognize me in the concrete ecotone, my bravado welling as Orion's terse face sinks behind smog, Artemis prowling elsewhere, the god of the sea sucking a shipwreck, don't / don't tell me it gets nicer when it's already nicer than I'd imagined, don't

or

don't tell me the stories of lonely femmes fucked by hidden gods, their costumes hilarious, feathered, sand, waves, a breathing canvas, a hot night, what pours off a god's body so akin to mine but less taxed, less commodity ruin / here, where beauty plays new notes on bad strings she says pin you, and I get pinned, over-lit, highly visible, traveling the road everyone must travel / a month elapses, how much does the horned god want me to give it up and to whom, I don't know / what

or

it's worth nothing, I tell my daughter, it's worth what it's worth to you, and you / cannot speak / that number / it seems anchored to you, but then it drifts, don't give it out / to men / I say here's my number and call me if you need a place to stay on the road and have you met / minotaurs, have you noticed how cramped the hearts of centaurs, have you seen sirens by the shoreline, a demeter weeping to the seabird who guards the door, have you seen the arrangement of / hands tipped up, wrists bent in a mystic supplication, palms receiving the stillpulsing tip of Orion's idle sword, I once / expected it to be sharp, but I know now it rends with heat, with hot deep presence, with thoughts I cannot think on my own, it rends by stretching my interior into the exterior, by rendering beauty beside its point / I give / my tender friends / whatever I have / and hope it is even a fraction of / the grace they're due, my anchor shifts so slightly this belief that every day / must include pain

Where sound forms a bowl in the green my beloveds congregate and tho a drone scripts threat overhead we reap balm ash damp clover it's true time has eighty feet of handwoven rope in its satchel

my tender friends make a list of what's missing, stretch out in new grass, old sun, bodies in the middle of embodied time performing the act of memory, a longing in the rough, in the warmest shaft / sunlight medicine doubling as poison, waiting for its homeopathic moment, creasing a reminder into each palm, open / your hand, what did you get I ask each friend, tell me how to do it, tell me how to remember our starry youth / the horned god points to a row of beautiful lambs and says: I was them, I was just like them / sleights a handful of numbers to call later, doubles time, creases time until it's layered, and calls each combination like a tally or a sentence, and / sometimes calls mine, but today / the afternoon stretches long and I turn to it my face scripted with mascara, patience, and decades of sympathy

or

an empathetic frequency emitting both sound and light in this demeter's palm, she's next / to me purring quietly against the knoll, her mouth a harbor, we've / wandered in from the road / is this someone's temple / outmoded / gods gather here in comfort and everyone agrees the owners of the bar are sweethearts, the japanese whiskey more special, the quail's egg steeped in ginger and soy tastes sunlit, too, my tongue steps behind velvet / wants nothing but the night's tongue / wants nothing but talking, begs for talking, wants nothing but all of you talking, I / can suddenly smell the desert on my tender friends' skin, the cold copper childhood, and the spark of the maul as it hits not the soft pine it expected, but hickory stump, rebar / anything / altered by some father's hand / there aren't any / fathers here today, raising their hands saying, me / my daughter, my bullfaced childlike tender friend / tender friends at the bar, laughing, their bodies moving at the exact pace of the earth's orbit, while I move on night's time, cold and planetary, and / have lost everything but this memory / and talking

or

finally / finally, I pull the chain to darken the room into celestial stuff, the faint whirr of streetlights, a weary redwood that doesn't belong here, mournful, distant, it considers our bodies through the window, mine / the ghost of its proserpine and the ghost of its years hence astride / you / there's a tenderer name for you on my tongue, I / want nothing but your field-drenched tongue, my mouth overflows with it as a horn that doesn't empty, whose roots are the sea, whose lip caught bright and wet in teeth a wave against a still-pleasant shore, the salt / lick it from me and still I cannot know what I taste like, I / ask my bullfaced tender friend whose baleful eye creases at the corner, a private laughter, I say we saw everyone today gather in the pasture on the the far side of the road that everyone must travel / into a hidden / hide / shade in shade / risking hand to sunlight for a memory apiece, no one could guarantee it would be happy / in the palm, a fragment of a star long cooled, I / couldn't remember the spells to names, I couldn't speak enough into each of their ears, tightly, my breath hitched as it always has, the gasp / that precedes knowing, I knew / I knew you, I put my hand to every shoulder, my palm cupping the ridged horn, my fingers describing an intimate gutter between blade and spine, and if I had a husband, I had him not, and if a bride, I outwore her, and if I were welcome, still I borrowed / every dime, a metaphor / I fill my phone with numbers / everyone here / has held death, a dry and still stone, has held death a hot clay bead behind each eye, in the crease between the eyes / my bullfaced tender friend, whose ring catches the sunlight / still / in whose eye there are both reflections and apertures, telling stones that tell the time and the story

or

I roll over the grass / the elders / don't mind if you go slack in a spell, the tender friends know you're on your back because you don't lie any longer, I don't / lie still, I admit it's sex / I admit sex / into my palm, a rain of memorable pearls, I / wonder which is your beauty and which your shame, I / wanted nothing but each of you ripe and risen, each of you talking directly against my tongue, your unblinking black salt tongues strewn with trying, they / left us here / the retiring gods, and we had / no reason not to stay when the spell lifted and the sun set, I / still I want nothing but your salt tongue pouring over me / your whisper that you needn't have whispered / everyone must travel, it is the gods' truth we all love, and the drone / our love / drones, it was you and me and our tender friends, and we could see where the sail lifted, but we could not see death

or

yet

Survey the demolishing current then in response feed the muscular fabric of love hand over hand far reaching skeins that silk the terrain and therein we don't get anxious to own each other any longer I just want to drive and talk all night and feel this landscape breathe in my overswell

I'm so nostalgic for the grayshot time we could readily walk through the veil, the time death was no prerequisite for getting down, the time we talked on telephones / under the tipped up starry bowl, in the grass, sand bowl, in the hollow of the sea god's iliac crest, I won't lie back / won't lie / I'm comforted by each tactile embrace, love's ripped arm about my shoulder, a spell against feelings, against my own ambition slingshot straight up into the night, to Orion's cool scowl, kiss not / don't kiss me now if you don't like it, I've had your tongue in mine, a deal to pass the night companionable, no inquiry, all query, the quarry deep maw of someone / else

or

my bullfaced tender friend palms / in a minotaur's palm, a great bowl of a grasp, a minotaur's own heart, big and throbbing, a set piece, I / take it on the tongue, I take it despite its heft, I / muscle / beating muscle, wordseeking worldbuilding muscle, vast muscle forged in a cold room by witch-poor persons, by no one, really, muscle that grew wild in the field and loose in the road according to only its own fibrous longings, I / take it / hot on the tongue and swill, more beauty more brutality, and swallow what I can, I'll take it / back with me, the road from desert to sea that everyone must travel, that only a few of us walk in reverse, I want / to drive it blazing, but I follow rigor and walk its ruts, witness each unlike life unfolding in its meters, not just forward and back, but also infinite weft to even more infinite warp, what am I / doing pausing by the gates to over there when I'm still / I'm still required here

or

lift my skirt, my back pressed into fast iron gates, my skin heated by abandon / abandoned lovers, lost things, press me / press me deeply into the moment before I have to return to / living at the edge of the road with my hand extended to travelers, offer and clutch, I cannot hold fast / enough lovers, enough daughters, enough of law and sacrifice / nothing / gets done in the sympathetic dark, tonight, put me instead in love's big arm and incant like you mean it, friends tell me / we have lived long enough, it's / safe to let loose my heart on you, and listen / this love is different from previous loves because now we're all dying / a dirge one sings to oneself, a / demeter is up early at the door, she doesn't want to come in, she wants to know if it's really the hour of living and what we'll do at dark with all that salt our weeping leaves behind, our / wounds, I can't bear / another wound / so say nothing / just pulse beside me, pulse inside me, my pulse ebbing against my need, I don't / need you to feel this / same coordinate, I need you to spell it out, I need to recite the spell of names, to give men and gods the same number at which to reach me, to spell my name out in the bowl's bonefresh gully, I press / press my bruise to / Orion's cold lip, he / heals me not and hurts me not / and knotted up against his thigh, I am / crossing the orbit of beauty's least known form

or

lift my body that wears the young cow's hide, rides like youth, and gives light jobs high on the / rise above the inn, the guests can't see me if they don't look back, and they don't / look, there, what am I doing with shade beauty, hanging out by myself wondering how my tongue got so stained with feeling / I saw my tender friends assembled on a blue screen, I saw numbers accumulate in spells and promises, not grand promises, nothing that protects me from / this belief that every day must include / pain / nothing / obliterating white memory wiping the present moment, gone static, gone still in the rush of huntblood / I hear / a wave / will crash tonight / the heavens, a wave of starjunk and haters come down the back of Orion's soft neck, my / throat, too, lifted / what could I do, but offer you things / what could you do, but / refuse me, I spiral and fill with needles, the dark needles that knit the night her angsty skirt, that knit your tongue to mine when you fall too long silent, that pierce the night through its blue hide, I won't / open my mouth to set you free, close my teeth to / I resolve to sit so very still, back to throne, back to thigh, back to pulsing muscle, as though I don't hear you, I / hear you, I just want to drive now

Don't say you love if that love will then try to exit the gates when I was unexpectedly released from the underworld I couldn't imagine an orpheus I couldn't float I could only cling to my home

when I died, I died of nothing, I died of someone else's transgression, I / didn't die, but feigned death, and so lied very still against the ground, until, by measures, I lied inside the ground / call my name when you come, I / was instructed and did, on arrival, call your name, your number, some little known formula that might open the gate, but nothing / no one stands there, not the harpy, no seabird at the sea god's rag cliff, and no one watching the bull fields, every / opening unguarded, go where you want they said, we don't pay you any longer / I went / into the deep ground that goes hot, then cool, hotter still, then dark / red / filled with indifference / the gates spread and the road from the desert to sea ran overhead, flawlessly, without me, I swam down / go down, I told my daughter, deep enough and you'll see the mark of every man, you'll see the god's honest truth, the weary jaw, its underside pulsing with your number, it recites you, it spells you your name, that's the thing about spells, anyone / can utter them

or

I knew salt to be effective, love to be slick, and my tender friends to have sweetened the wine / was poison, too, and life, it was red, by turns, and white as the hospital sheet I wound / my lip, I wound my tongue, in my tongue was cradled a hunter's, heavy velvet drape of her, I / rang the bell on the gate / there, Orion was lost and never thought my name, again, did he

or

Artemis struck a star for me, I swore the name of the horned god and held my hands cupped in case anything poured forth / my friend who offered me this fat grave stilled me / still me / make me quiet as a shade / grove / find my rundown clock abandoned, my phone abandoned, the last day of equinox tasting bitter, don't let it surprise you

or

there are dogs, here, I can't see them, but they scent me with the belief that every day must contain / contain me / my bullfaced tender friend cannot contain me, the gods of sea and sky and one-hundred songs aren't here to contain me, I'm loose about the field / what's so soft beneath my palm must feel even softer under rough touch, a dido / raises a hammer, pounds on the gates / pounds / bangs me out, banged against the gate, and, one day, they'll bang me back into service, the cracked screen of what once was precious, a strange gift / I had to see / each face and, then, each face as each tender friend had seen it, but no one had / visited my grave / my grave / countenance, I / wasn't officially dead, pop music played from my speaker, my nipples went purple with cold and, with age, I became the perfect shade, don't think / a horned proserpine / could hold her own / hand over her own mouth, for long, don't think I could've quieted / down under the earth

or

a hades fucks me and I shrug, it's a transaction, an oily trial / takes place over decades, what / are the chances, I ask justice, and justice shrugs, a noisy show of plates and chain / give me, instead, your rope, bind me, instead, behind this gate and I swear to you I will finally die / the witch gets held down by a stone, a succubus by a stone / one's history spelled out in stones across the surfaceworld itself a stone, beauty, even, a stone carved still and quiet / to talk is to murder beauty, and I was made of talking

or

I was unmade by talking, I spoke and disturbed the desert, I spoke and the sea begrudged me, I spoke / more than / wept / called out your names as I was coming / along the path, that ran along the road everyone must travel, it wasn't visible, but I could / smell the asters and the poppies, I could see leaf-green beetles and pale iguanas all muscle and bleach wearing the path deeper into quartz, I could see salt shimmer in each direction and know that none of those were the direction I traveled, I / found the place the plants assigned us and sank down into the grainy sand, then dirt, then root, then muck, I / found my skirt hitched to the gate, I swore the name I spelled when it was a tender friend's, a god in a tender friend's skin, just / always a ruse, I / rose from death in four-hundred days, I owed money and time and no longer remembered / if I'd had a husband, he mourned me / if a bride, I was no longer young, my / daughter was grown and signed in her own hand a lease, a risk, I couldn't lift my eyes to her face, I couldn't say the name of the door I wished to enter / again, my home / it wasn't the desert, the sea, the road, the ditch, the / grove contained me not / my friend held me not in that great palm, my tender friends let go the sail, and when the god of the sea all loosed with pearl and froth called my name, it wasn't familiar, it was business

or

come here and show me the ring long through your nose, your velvet nostrils
flared in thought, show me your thinking hand on the screen, it prints and
spells my name, I think / for some long years about that gold circle, perhaps
/ never threaded with rope and chain, perhaps it was a rare glint, you / rode
afield, the only one of my tender friends who looked more forward than back,
I / didn't look / I talked and my hands were ruined, I talked a ruined speech,
I spelled / out / of space and time for several thousand hours, was I missed /
Orion! the Or, the O, the open edge of the gate against the open edge of the
grave against my open mouth, and, with his ice cold tongue, plant there the
answer you want me to speak, I'm / quiet now and I will

Hold my wrist hold my ankle hold my tongue hold my mouth in your mouth and tell me things singular and windcrossed tell me murder and tell me future they're spelled the same

the things I touched turned less to gold, more to game, an / underworld stain coaxed bright, they felt my touch a wave of starry yes / I was standing by the side of the road that runs from desert to sea, a pair of iguanas pinking my ankles, a desert bee, a white-lined sphinx moth in my hair as though in history, a songbird the cats had stunned, a willow blossom, a breeze from the hottest, most eastern body / in the desert sky, I saw carved the summer warning, the risk of another year unfolding, unfamiliar / hands, palms up, offering some invisible boneshare, I had long been drinking from strangers' palms, I wasn't afraid of what they carried, but / how they would leave / me / my arm about my young friend's shoulder, happy young friend, her love all in view, and, my tender friends, you know what it's like when your love's all in view

or

bring me some diana whose selenite glow isn't the violent seascape of illness and absence, she goes / red at the edges, gold at the center, silver inside, she has blue veins and green salt eyes that speak a language, her stone lip gray, unyielding hums, she calls the travelers' numbers, names, their musk notes in notebooks torn from their hands and tossed caszh back at their feet / everyone must travel this road, but not everyone will stop over and bide with me / overbide, read me the note the moon drew out of you, read me what you wrote before you got here, and, later, after you've left, send me hot word, I / also know the spell for coming and going / home, beckoning my tender friends who lived somewhere deep and damp and cloud, I checked the phone they lit, we're lit af they said and it's possible af they said, and I felt almost a part of the chorus

or

meet me after you fuck, after I say siltsex things in the heavens' dark ear, and / after the worst of my faults have sent up their charge, the ground shifts and the sand settles, no flower here minds the creosote giving ancient face, I / go down / on the horned god, an elbow in the ribs, my hair tangled, calcium hide / out / pour white-lined sphinx moths, signing away my underworld name, frozen moths holding repose, a replica of my wonderface, I / spoke the horned god's favorite spell, I said O and left my breath in my throat, caught / catch / the rope flung over the raw edge of the grave, the gate, its hem raveling / shot from Artemis's bow, thrown over Orion's steadily receding shoulder, my wrist through its eye, say: the rope has no master, say: no one owns whoever's tied to this rope, no one owns me, so no one pays for me, nor my rent / garments / the food I eat, topside hungry

or

each crucial hour gets spent shaded, weeps slowly, then evaporates, I / don't love life I / say, my tender bullfaced friend says: bury life, says: here is the stone and the crossed wires, wraps my wrist until, electric, we admit the belief that every day must contain pain and / stop / I say the spell for still and stop / so still me / be my stone and cross me deep and put me back in the ground, hold me, just there, while fear draws my bath, and I / fearbate my heart / feel its undying, I'm / hesitant to read or, worse, to shush, I'm talking a wall around my bed, tonight / I neither walk the road, nor answer the phone, I / give you the sign that says not a moment spent here will ever you leave empty, drink a bright holy wine, and sleep until you know yourself, I'll / meet you there, if maybe I can

My tender friend thinks I live dangerously but says no it's not the breast full of scorpions nor the lack of income it's the way I leap into the arms of the gods sure they'll catch me no I say I'm not sure I'm never sure

I don't draw a card for the capricorn moon, I draw a breath, I breathe cautiously through nettle mask, breath shallow so as not to disturb the fiberglass, asbestos, dogs, men, I / breathe the crease between thigh and trunk, I get pressed in the crease of a trunk, it's the only way out of the desert, a leaden shield I wear, a silence I produce to inhibit a deep chill, I / impersonate, my daughter says: where are we going, it / isn't polite, I tell her, to ask the destination, it's okay not to know where / you're going next / might be a wreckscape, might be a wicked place, might have men for dogs and dogs for men, my / friends won't be there / I'll be the only demeter / the only philomel / the only proserpine, horned, ivied, or otherwise, if I / had a pain like this for the first time, would I think I was dying

or

I want things to be magical, but have a hard time inhabiting magic / where the road from the desert to the sea stretched was magic, but it didn't touch me, it or I couldn't, I / could see cold planets while all around me there was heat, I could see prehistoric fauna while all around me cars and fences, I couldn't stand / I couldn't / ran / ran hard out on the road everyone must travel so many times, I'd never get mortal, so where to now I asked the hunters, still and steady, sword for a spine, bow for breast, sometimes / I get nowhere, my tender friends text me from those places they go / pain would follow, I've / heard that / every day / must include / the raving fear that there will be no further income, no redemptive occupation, everything / flows out, I / am a series of lettings go, ungrasping, that is, I breathe continuously, but not very well

or

do not attribute your pain to anything other than living topside where pain is a basic unit of personhood, a sedimentary layer that makes itself known through discrete vehicles, bodies, a topography and ontology, but also always only ever pain / that every day must include in its catalogue / must not include, necessarily, reprieve, need / not include reassurance, need not include

My bullfaced tender friend was right about everything I consume one nasturtium after another wishing I'd been alive when first found

but I wasn't / I was / somebody else's eurydice and my friend had none, no bride, though sirens mobbed and mopped that great ridged brow and stole that steady breath and laughed deep throated laughs, their thighs around that great torso, as mine would be, hands braced against horns, the horned god above and below, singing come on kids, come on kids, I / wasn't a kid any longer, not a bride or groom myself, nor anything we give a livid name / anyone / for whom an incantation would be / enough / my bullfaced tender friend incanted, and / I rose / that's the entire story, though I'll tell you more, I / was selfish insofar as I had a self, selfless insofar as I lived outdoors on the road everyone must travel, I / was work, I was labor with a blunt shovel / dig me up from the underworld, draw my grave a gold circlet and the thousand hours it takes you

or

love me, but only after the fact, love me only when I'm walking out of the sea for the last time, the sea god casting eyes on my tears and ass in equal appraisal, city light against my profile, my lips radiant another year or two, my promise not to fall in love well kept on the surface, and hollow as any abandoned shell on the sea god's ugly fucking crown, it's / okay to wear some nasty halo and call yourself a demon, shake out your tail over a brash wave in a hot sea, it's okay to feel seven different types of love, the seventh tangled in your braids, a seven-pointed starry heaven / at least from there, I am never exiled / Orion doesn't love me, but he owes me one, so I climb his regal sword, you / wouldn't know it, crusted as it is with regret, but I know he was a princess before the hunt did him in / I was a princess, too, we came from the eastern hills, and wore our hair to our narrow waists in fast leather and slow time, I / thought we'd last long enough for me to die, that is, I thought I'd lived my whole life

or

it's the tears that turn you to salt, it's a metaphor, what they mean is whoever looked back at her, whichever wife she was that saw disappointment, she wept till salt were more than flesh gone dull with / his arm in the night slung over, heavy, he used to work outside, he / says: is that what you call it / Orion / I ask about shapeshifters, I guess I didn't believe Orion could get meaty, I thought each star a salt crystal on a string, hot, the connective tissue cold and smart between them / I thought him an intelligence I was not prepared to / become his wife, he called me demeter, my phone lit up, he called me demibird, love, good girl, rolled his thumb against my prism, and salt, he called my name / who would I have been if I didn't respond / when finally Orion spoke / was it no one

or

I'm already home, I've already arrived, I say dear one, dear Orion, I made my home in your boot and let you tread me all these years as though I were water, as though you left the sky just to bathe in me, a hunter rinsing off the blood and sweat, a thinker rinsing a stubborn thought, but never did I think in my salt you'd still dwell, I / thought myself a hunter, too, but am I sky or dirt

I ducked into a sympathetic pleiades and before I knew it neither desert nor sea stopped where the mountains started

I call a moira for the news, she says you have to want to live, you have to want it, I don't / argue it's time to spend the last egg, it's time to sell every hot rock out from under the fire / god of the sea gives me a shove and Orion will hardly know I'm gone, that little pressure behind his ear as I whisper see ya / I see you, I / tune out the pleasure dome with a well-placed teardrop on its wick, and / tell me whose number is that / my screen writhes, I / don't even flinch / wtf / text me, wtf / it's understandable, the news breaks our stride, the news is more travelers due, and suddenly I can't extend my hand into the road from desert to sea everyone must travel, another / child's face in my hands, another dusty child, not mine, my daughter / asks where do they go, I say it isn't polite to ask destinations, I / remember the first-time clang of the gates, my skirt stiff, rusted in its hinge / my own hinge raking loud, a curved spine / a curvedspine hour, tangled tailbone in minutes, placed off-center, a sleepy child's face, I can't go with you, I have to tell her

or

I have a new name, now, it came to me in a text message / if you wake up with dirt on your tongue, it's me / if you wake up with blood stains and sand, if you wake up, wake me up and rinse your curls in the fountain, whistle my call, molar, round, an emptied-out safe, and palm full of tack, I'm / making a list of contracts I've gotta ditch, I / think in a circle in the hottest part of the road, I keep my toe in this circle in the hot road, in a pure coin of light, in a dry, animal breath, a gust of spines and fine stones, the last aster crisp, the pack rats tucked under three centuries of cholla and industry, there's a catapult, a library, a waterfall, anything you can picture in surprise canyon, in the fourth of july mountains, in the trailer hauled out here by no means / no

or

borrowed time comes due and the phone gets bright with intent, the engine turns back time, unfolds the desert as far back east as it can, then further back, mountains intervene through a rigid sheet of tears, salt-thick and brittle, loose / magic spills from my pockets, it's time / to admit there's no orpheus, no money, no harp, no home, no hearth, no hope / an electric storm coalesces where my core was, where my heart stopped to regard you / and then started again, I had to leave fast to keep pace with it, I had to

Do not acknowledge you love lest it claw from you your body where I live in the desert but am always wet I wept for my home just a hole

the sky seems wrong tonight, tilted, spilling its letters starskew, where / are the hunters, I see only sisters, cups of clean cool water, bears, I see the seat of knowledge, the throne of the sisters, their chariot, a lance, is that Orion's sword, he's / gone, I take his belt and wrap it many times around my bare waist, here, where being alive is sexy enough, no one needs / elastic, sculpted, tended beasts of the field, all doe of eye and velvet tongue, all golden volume and hardon sequence, I don't / anyhow / we're going to a darkened glade, the clouds roll in over the moon, not new, but weak, the storm can't commit / murder wind whips up, our phones won't glow, they're dead and a hades who / did he think he was that he could call my number and my name would respond with my voice, my laugh, was I something he remembered flush with feeling, still replete, north in moneytown with my rings on and no / worries, I scarred myself happily to remember our night for some long time before it was my lot to walk the road everyone must travel / whatever / the weather tonight, waning moths, bottle flies, iridescent green, transparent memory

or

I can never say how we met / is she very pretty, a friend asks, don't you know / what I look like changes / I look like change, arcana-time death comes up, again, one more bone from the hole I'm boning, my / phone rings, I entered an incantation in place of your name, it's easier to greet a slew of stars, black hearts, skulls, wind, pocket full of quartz like teeth, pocket full of teeth, small bones I grew and grafted, gave and got back like gifts / that is, when the god of the hunt gives you a fight, it is a weapon, don't let it get turned on / you, an arrow, you / an arrow's vane, and me, its converged steel, perfect thief tip through the skin, as quietly as a virus through the heart, as slim as any belief / each day / must contain / a death / I hear about it on the news, I wait for its traveler to come strange down the road / everyone must travel / some friends must travel sooner than others, young / golden face in my hands, white teeth in my pocket, red lips, whose / teeth are these, I'm / not their mother / when you find the child's teeth in your palm, you must find the mother, but this doesn't happen / to you / I like it better on the desert side, where there are very few buildings, few things built to be the world that mock it instead / I think meadow, I go meadow when I'm in a building, I breathe, hoping for the flower scent that leads to my bullfaced tender friend, it's safe in that great shadow / unlike / most shade

or

I talk the sun up and down and up again about love, and still don't think it's a boring word, I say love, I print it on my knuckles, it'll scar my friend says / demeter where have you been, I'm in the meadow again, where are you, shade / falls from yew, willow, an olive tree green with sudden gasp out of the grave, cruel return, no warning, who / wintered here, whose tooth, what traveler out of sorts circling its base, who wasn't meant to pass you / on the road / only some things travel both ways: creosote, memory / lapses into cloudburst, and the desert swims further east of the sea, no / no god of the sea allowed, no / no returns, no / no ticket window, no train, one rail, diverted ties rot, I'm yanking loose boards and soaking rusty nails in seawater to make the stain / mark the road, nothing stays / no story, no symbol, no eye, no house, no bowl safe enough, but still / guests stay the night, it isn't polite to ask their destination I tell my daughter, shhhhhh, check their bags, check for huntknives, for names, for words spelled differently, you / remember worlds were once spelled / differently

or

it hurts me to see my daughter remember, I / hold her teeth in my pocket quietly, I know these teeth were first mine, then they hurt her / the day is over and I can't be kind, wouldn't / be fair / be kind / be very pretty, a sunset a cholla blossom filled with a bee's work, a bee's body, hard, I hum, too, a demeter hums a minor / miner / we know the salt mine never closes, but none of the miners can see me, they're facing the sea, all / my tender friends, face a pleiades of regrets all night, they face a charred altar, it's how / there is no time

or

there is no time I wasn't careening down scree through turnstiles, laughing mouthful of cometstail, anyhow, a minotaur was there, the ring through their muzzle catching light on the opposite platform, no one knew / where the light came from, maybe it was in them like a bloom that after dusk unravels and its petals, a secret set of bands, a secret set of snakes, a rattling beware, a poison, the wrong apple / brings me back to life too early, I'm both this memory and a living / thing / hold me / tell me what you told our tender friends about me, and make it sweet, I'm not yet sold / on living

Hurts to arrive in you and hurts to go you made me softer than I was a habitable dirt for all sorts of flourish I'm not hating on salvations I'm just calling out

replicate this fifty-mile canyon stretch of the road from sea to desert along an untrenched artery / I've grounded, until now, my breastplate / slack, my heart, that I might traverse the road unseen / end scene / still / just / sitting here / common bride of states and sweethearts, I'll belong under anyone for an hour, I'll change my life for anyone, why not, I made / everything / pictures, you wondered, did I keep / anything to myself, you're funny, I kept everything, the real shots I text my tender bullfaced friend, I have your crushed petals here in the glovebox protected in the gloved palm where the glove tears thumb from pink cuss, like I would do you / if I'd been there, a protection spell, maybe / it's okay to be a demeter with her glass half full, it's okay to admit I've got something left / out in the shallow where sea goes clearer than sky, the surf god isn't so bad, seals lounge barking, wryly clapping, rolling off into the day waves, bye, I hold your hand at the rust-hollowing rail on the graycore path, sunandblood flecked, that runs the cliff to the road, the road itself, the flower from which we snort a bee / my hand slipped, I would do it, I would do every transgress twice to meet you

or

I would not live anywhere, now / I try to be home for my children / I am already every fiber of you, I tell them / the threat, the truth, the promise / I tell them some things about the canyon and it / the word canyon / sounds to me as big as it's meant to / how can anyone walk down the exact center, the salt bleeding out to either side, I / square my thighs, center my thighs / over / I'm throat-first, I'm mouth, my tender friend reminds me to look up when I'm devouring / I don't look up, until / locks my eye, a silver key clinking down the back of my throat, are we serious / I don't know / in covelets, cloven kids whisper happy blonde things, I'm / sorry I tell my daughter / who knows / what she has / coming / coming to in the desert, I've got the spells, I'm dizzy with the spell of my tender friends' names, a runaway kid, free beast, field thing, a thing I've never been so big those scars seem monuments, then later I'm just a cut-up / Orion doesn't laugh, but he knows I'm funny back here in the desert alone on the roof, a hot current of meaning making it motelhard to remember, were we / serious / I don't know, was I fun / a good time, barefoot on black widows, too sunlazy to believe in anything, too sour, too, to admit I don't live here / is to admit I'm unhinged / no stake or screw in my back to still me, arched out of bed, wall, floor, counter, rough old carpet, push me through the surface on which you'll love / love me and / if it's the sea surface, let it be full of foam, homegirl steady, a lot of rainbows before I kick out / no one promised to preserve me back to shore, the scratchy red rope, it's in my hand, anyway, sliding through crushed petals, smells of sex, safe houses, thighseam, sometimes I just want to wake up and give you everything! I'm shouting / sometimes up the road thinking you might hear me from this inane distance, can't everyone hear / crash my party, I beg, crash the length of me, I can feel the exterior muscle that powers your arm around your beloved, drunk with touching you / don't / make me stop / I'll leave soon, anyhow, just the screen lit up in my wake, hot reprieve

Free salmacis from bodies not hers and free the mirror from its rocky wall and free the sand from its bound service grief a pearl my wealth is pearls then they dissolve

give a poor salmacis a break, each body I see, I leap into, typical naiad, I just need to check out of personhood's bleak blaring motel, maybe / I'm just here for contrast / high / I checked into this fountain whose lobby was the sea god's home, opened the door guarded by horseshoes and mantas, by a seabird and what are there but mirrors, I / sat topless for hours, who knows if gods even return home, but I knew how to get in and go deeper into the following locations: reflections, selfies, profile pics, the water, soft sides, bed and bed and bed, again, in the era of looking / for something in the mirror / bloodred and hasty, I needed to be no, no one, numb, it was a democracy of misplacement, the names I usually called out slurred with names I didn't yet know, the names I was going to need very soon, I / lay myself down saying go, please go / grainy fountain and gone-pale food, sex and coffee pot, posts I don't know how to / feel anything / I'm saying I feel a coldred ghost where there used to be a lot of / time / welling up, thoughts indistinct from vanes, feathered thoughts, soft until fired where / was Artemis who'd come to dinner, I / looked into the sea god's mirrors where they lined up with the night sky, in the fountain where a fat fish refused fortune, in the fish's belly, in its score of bones that read like leaves, and then I looked online for her / be / my tender friend / there / I want you to stand, another apex joining silk route to silk root, the moths cut so, and spilled from cocoons, ravel me, I / want you to web my center out to the horizon, please

or

I can't check out, I'm wasting so much money every time I roll over, we're that much closer to the edge, my / children don't go hungry, yet / I'm the demeter who will get everything wrong in time / never / get it all wrong at once / don't travel the road from desert to sea more than once if you want to die a proper death / the gristle of feeling ebbing off into smudge with your name and your bee's breath, there / are too many hummingbirds between the door and the gate, too many messengers, all messages a type of blood / type / every letter I type into my phone slips loose and pools / my own reflection is penitentiary enough for one life, don't make me go in there / my tender friends don't make me go / on

or

I sat topless for hours, the cheer of my body multiplied fantastically far back into the sea god's home scared me not, where / was the muscle, where were the musclecold dancers, troupe Artemis, all action, and arms up, arms up, when you lay a body down with arms up, the arms reach / when you lift a body up, the arms trail / when you wrap her arms around you, find yourself inside and wonder if this were the room you meant to check into, this solution / check a box that changes your whole premise / check the right box, and suddenly

or

pretty-horned and ivy-skeined, those dappled things that make a face, the warm look when the moon is blue and the screen is blue and no one sleeps for either sight, I / can't really see my bullfaced tender friend in here, who's too big for mirrors, decked in petals, salt streaming from hide and horns pointed north, turning away, and from behind, seafoam laps those great temples, who / is it who turned to seafoam last, I wonder, was it actually the prince, was it a mother tracking her child from the desert to the sea, the / demeters say we aren't sovereign, yet, aren't sated this night, the night a knife-nicked artery / and again and again / this heavy night with its swollen moon dragged down in the sky, a roaring wrong lot of blood, hands from all directions, defensive wounds, on a night like this / it isn't right to answer the phone or to think about how to get out of a body and back into a self / it isn't right when these babes get turned to coldred foam and washed out, spit out by hate and spit in the eye of hate and spit in the sea where it makes a merry sound of sibling / hood my tender friends, I won't lose track of a single one of you, though the shore is far and sea on the rise

With all their space compressed such that they are purestar hunters they can be stretched inside me I envelope them a red envelope of radical dust

An old chiron comes by, his lips blue, his arms tattooed with burned down fragments, ash creeping up his collar, his mouth ash, his feet wheels, his oar through his neck, he comes home not because he expects me to be here / he doesn't / remember my name / he comes by and sleeps in my bed without asking, bares his teeth at me, intruder / I am / not getting / in the bed, I go out and look up the dome so empty somehow, I always think I'll be big enough, I'm never big enough, my / daughters are grown, now, my sons, brides of nothing but the plastic rings that held time / it's gone, every everywhere, gone, I go / to the sea and the god of the sea is richcold, an eel skin I / go to the desert and the creosote speaks kindly, I don't know

or

that empty bed, the dome, so fast there's / no one to be patient / be patient with me, I say to my tender friends, it's time to treat me like a person, even if I'm not one / quite yet / I say / but everyone's asleep and I'm short on tears / my daughter breaks an egg, you're a woman now, daughter, break your own eggs, I tell her / it's alright to watch me love a dying body of stars, I was / made for this / and then it's night on the road where a coyote moves like a soldier, crisp turns, she takes turns with a black dog I can see only by his tongue / his tongue lights the road / for a moment / I think I should go back to the house, see if the chiron's still breathing, see if my daughter has stuck a spine through his heart / she always wished men were sturdier / see if my children have given their children's bodies to the future, they want / to be a wave of time coasting out over every arborescent hope

or

Orion finally steps down from the sky, one cold boot after the other hits the hills where the banshee with the head of a dog roams, her mistress above, she lets him pass because one cold boot after the other / his hunter's vest, planetary furs, and his own dog beside him, his ghost of dogs, he / wears the kind of roses that grow in the gap between stars, that is, he / plays a hidden chord / made of time and matter / he's our-sized, now, and has my number, I see / my phone glow and when I hit the wash there's Orion standing in a blue light / around him, the bones of people who got too tired to make it back to town, to finish walking the road, we'll / carry them out later / later / a coyote's leg, too, it's rough and lonesome / left there by some tide, what / is he doing here, what are you doing here, I ask

or

I've been crying, but Orion can't tell, he's / flesh, now, still when he greets me, a perseid cascade, his belt undone, his sword down by the riverside / what used to be a river, then a wash / a wash of sand forgetting a wash of heat, even / in the winter you can feel the hot tide, even / at night in January at the start of another person's year

or

I know it, but it's from a book and I'm not, I'm from / this book / this road everyone must travel / just because it ends doesn't mean the road ends, I walk it back there to the sea, I nod and the crests of palms silt the road / the rain weeps in as though there were more air, and the salt is the same at either end of the canyon, the valley, the notch, the crest / the crest of Orion's hips, over his belt, the crest of a lightning bolt, I / didn't think there was electricity in the stars, I say, I thought it was a myth, it is a myth, he says: like you are / he has a crevasse between one side of his ribcage and the other, the gap between stars, and it pulses, a gap in my memory, pulses, says, one time something cold loved you

or

something cold, I start a fire in the wash, I build up old mattresses, chair legs, and bottles, even glass will burn here if you give it a reason, I tell Orion, but he's looking the other way for a horse that often comes by, I think / I hear its hooves at night and know it's also a coyote / we each are, in addition to what we used to be / a loose pack, our hair, fur, tangled, our mouths ready, our teeth as good as they need to be to / hope our hope

or

I don't want to trust anyone, to spend any time lying in anyone's arms, to have a name anyone slips in my ear, I / don't want my numbers to make sense, I don't want to calculate the damages, the damaged things, we toss them out in the wash, I / tell my lawyer, check the wash, check by the coyote's leg, tell me how a leg washes up alone, without / a demeter tells me how the rest of us washed up here, a mercury comes by and I can't even call, a venus comes by and I can't even / name on my tongue calls us to the fire and gives us the only story I can really stand, mother winter, who gives a mouthful of jewels to any child who doesn't balk, but gives a pheasant's talon to anyone who does, then / demeter sticks a match in the book

or

there's a cord with intentions wicking just beyond the glass, a chord that sits between frets, fret work, and something strung along the gap between stars, all as old as the thousand-year-old lights of / my tender friends, they tell me it's going to be / fucking okay / they tell me I'm in love and I say yeah most of the time / they don't know I'm hanging up the stars, they don't know I'm hanging out in a bed of stardust and strings, wearing my hair down, changing my name, again, counting my / blessings, or, as we call them in legal terms, damages / I'm so cool, most nights / Artemis shows me how to feel those things that aren't supposed to breathe in the stars and get close enough to taste, now / flesh, puts a palm on my stomach, I breathe all the way in, I breathe all the way, and then breathe out / fire and salt burst from the dark dome of sweet night, in winter, in the desert, on the road, I'm / going home, I say and I don't know if it's / there

Acknowledgments

Poems from the manuscript appear in *APR, BAX Best American Experimental Poetry 2019, Bear Review, Big Other, Burning House, Ilanot Review, Milk Press, The New South, Ocean State Review,* and *The Tiny*.

Some adjectives in this text come from or are inspired by *The Homeric Hymns*.

The seabird comes from André Breton's *My Heart Through Which Her Heart has Passed*.

"I turned thirty in wartime I turned forty in wartime stay you irritate my heart with distance until the present comes a sheet of pearls and moor's breath in a dry clime and I bedeck you" mentions Moacyr Scliar's book *The Centaur in the Garden*.

"Everyone tells me there's no work on this road I make bad choices okay fine but I swing from a godswell and take a punch like a philomel" is in conversation with the fairy tale projects of Lara Glenum, Lily Hoang, and Sabrina Orah Mark, among others.

"I fall asleep waiting for a call from the tribunal waiting for the elders to get here with their sacrificial blade I fall asleep before I die I want more dreams" contains a paraphrase from PJ Harvey's "No Girl So Sweet."

The phrase *cold and planetary* comes from Sylvia Plath's "The Moon and the Yew Tree."

"With all their space compressed such that they are purestar hunters they can be stretched inside me I envelope them a red envelope of radical dust" shares a connection with Rosebud Ben-Oni's "{turn around}" from her book *Bright XYXS*.

Thanks to Chelsea Biondollilo and her book *The Skinned Bird: Essays* for introducing me to *the bare spot on a bird's chest* through which taxidermists make their incisions.

Thank you to Sarah Vap.

Thank you to the Bloof Books NaPoWriMo crew and Shanna Compton in particular, thank you to my tender friends and my children. Thank you to Hoa Nguyen, Timothy Liu, and everyone at Saturnalia Books. Thank you to CAConrad and Erika Meitner. Thank you to Rochester Institute of Technology for the leave it supported.

About the Author

Danielle Pafunda is author of ten books of poetry and prose, including winners of Ricochet Editions' Troubling the I contest and the Saturnalia Books Poetry Prize selected by Hoa Nguyen. Pafunda has also published two chapbooks and many poems, essays, stories, and hybrid works in journals and anthologies such as *American Poetry Review*, *BAX: Best American Experimental Writing*, *Conjunctions*, *Hick Poetics*, *Pleiades*, and *The Texas Review*, and appeared in poetics performances in venues like University of Southern California's Visions and Voices and &Now. She/they teach creative writing, worldbuilding, literature, and gender and queer studies at Rochester Institute of Technology.

Also by Danielle Pafunda

Spite

The Book of Scab

Beshrew

The Dead Girls Speak in Unison

Manhater

Natural History Rape Museum

Iatrogenic

My Zorba

Pretty Young Thing

Along the Road Everyone Must Travel was printed in Adobe Garamond Pro
www.saturnaliabooks.org

www.ingramcontent.com/pod-product-compliance
Lightning Source LLC
Chambersburg PA
CBHW030532080526
44586CB00011B/409